Chemical Reactions

Jenna Winterberg

Consultant

Brent Tanner
Mechanical Engineer

Publishing Credits

Rachelle Cracchiolo, M.S.Ed., *Publisher*
Conni Medina, M.A.Ed., *Managing Editor*
Diana Kenney, M.A.Ed., NBCT, *Content Director*
Dona Herweck Rice, *Series Developer*
Robin Erickson, *Multimedia Designer*
Timothy Bradley, *Illustrator*

Image Credits: p.4-5 iStock; p.8-13 iStock; p.15 iStock; p.16 © Universal Images Group Limited/Alamy.jpg p.17 (Illustration) UIG via Getty Images, (background) iStock; p.21 iStock p.22 GIPhotoStock/Science Source; p.23 Charles D. Winters/Science Source; p.24-26 iStock; p.27 (top, bottom right) © sanapadh/Alamy; p.28-29 (illustrations) Timothy Bradley; all other images from Shutterstock.

Library of Congress Cataloging-in-Publication Data

Winterberg, Jenna, author.
  Chemical reactions / Jenna Winterberg.
  pages cm
  Summary: "Dynamite is highly explosive. This is because it's a chemical reaction waiting to happen. Many things go through chemical reactions. When you cook or eat, a chemical reaction takes place. Understanding chemical reactions will not only keep you safe, it will also help reveal the world around you."-- Provided by publisher.
  Audience: Grades 4 to 6
  Includes index.
  ISBN 978-1-4807-4724-1 (pbk.)
  1. Chemical reactions--Juvenile literature.
  2. Chemistry--Juvenile literature. I. Title.
  QD501.W722 2016
  541.39--dc23
                                        2015003015

Teacher Created Materials

5301 Oceanus Drive
Huntington Beach, CA 92649-1030
http://www.tcmpub.com

ISBN 978-1-4807-4724-1

Table of Contents

Everyday Chemistry

When we think of chemistry, it's hard not to picture a lab with students wearing coats and goggles and using flasks and burners. But chemistry doesn't just happen in school. It regularly occurs all around us.

Take breakfast, for example. Maybe you ate an egg or a piece of bread. Those foods are created through chemistry. And the way your body takes those foods and turns them into energy is another example of chemistry at work. In these cases, it's a **chemical reaction**. In other words, a change takes place that alters the material's makeup. The raw egg changes when it's scrambled or boiled. The food changes when your body digests it.

Chemical reactions are such a normal part of our lives that we hardly note when they take place. We take for granted that when we put gas in our cars, it will fuel them. We don't think about science when we bake cookies or cakes. And chemistry is the last thing on our minds when we're warming ourselves by a wood-burning fire, watching fireworks up in the sky, or admiring the changing colors of autumn leaves. But without chemical reactions, none of these things would happen.

Combining Substances

Fresh cookies don't just appear out of thin air. (Don't we wish!) You have to combine ingredients first before you bake them. For any chemical reaction, you need ingredients. In this case, we call them **reactants**, because they are going to react to a **chemical change**. In baking, reactants are things such as sugar, eggs, and flour. But they could be just about anything: from oxygen or water to copper or salt.

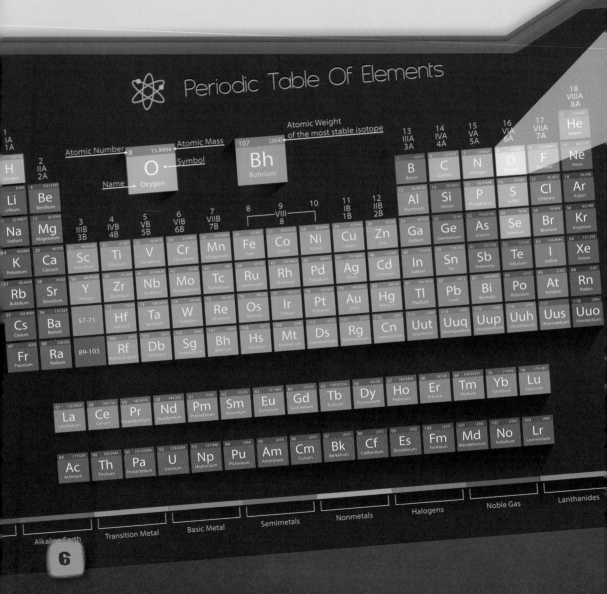

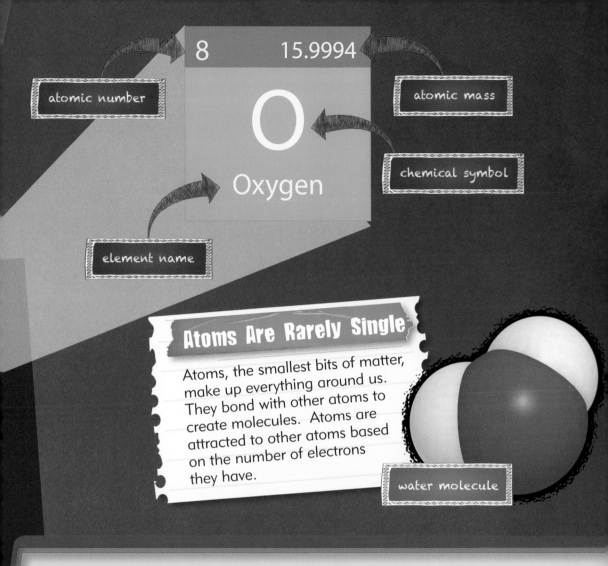

8   15.9994

O
Oxygen

atomic number

atomic mass

chemical symbol

element name

Atoms Are Rarely Single

Atoms, the smallest bits of matter, make up everything around us. They bond with other atoms to create molecules. Atoms are attracted to other atoms based on the number of electrons they have.

water molecule

The simplest form of a reactant is an **element**. An element is a substance that contains only one kind of atom. For example, oxygen is an element. Water is made up of two kinds of elements: oxygen and hydrogen. When two or more elements bind together like this, the result is a **compound**. Compounds can be reactants, too.

There are far too many compounds to list them all. But the number of elements is limited. We make sense of them by way of a chart called the *periodic table*.

The chart organizes the elements by atomic number. That's the number of protons in each atom. It also contains the atomic mass—the number of protons plus the number of neutrons.

Chemical reactions don't happen every time two substances combine. Sometimes, the combinations simply form mixtures. In these cases, a **physical change** occurs—not chemical.

A physical change can affect the way a substance looks—such as its size, shape, or color. Sugar will dissolve in water. When combined, they form a type of mixture called a *solution*. But the sugar and water have not changed chemically. In fact, they can still be separated.

Plain cookie dough is another solution. You've mixed flour, sugar, butter, eggs, and other things to make the dough. This mixture would be difficult, but not impossible, to separate. Still, no chemical change has taken place.

All gas mixes are solutions. Take the air we breathe. It contains oxygen, sure. But it also has other elements such as nitrogen and compounds such as carbon dioxide. There are a total of 15 gases in our air!

Solutions are just one kind of mixture. They're homogeneous. In other words, all of the parts are evenly mixed and completely spread out. You can't see or tell one part from another. Your plain cookie dough is a homogeneous mixture. Other mixtures are heterogeneous. They contain a little more of one part than another. You can easily see the different parts of the mixture. If your cookie dough had pieces of chocolate that you could see (or even pick out!), it would be heterogeneous.

A Sweet Alternative

A colloid is a special type of homogeneous mixture. It has larger particles than a solution, but they are still evenly spread out.

Tricky Mixing

A mixture can always be separated. If it can't, then a chemical reaction has taken place. Even solutions such as sugar dissolved in water can be separated. Simply boil the water until you are left with just the sugar. Sometimes, it just takes a special tool. So, think hard before you say that your mixture can't be reversed!

heterogeneous

homogeneous

Examining Properties

When we combine substances, we want to know what changes. We get this data by observing and measuring. You might note that a mixture is pink in color. That's a good observation! But would it mean more if you knew the colors of the original substances? If they were white and red, pink is no surprise. But if they were white and blue, it's an exciting result!

To make sense of mixtures, we need to understand individual parts first. That's why we measure and observe before *and* after.

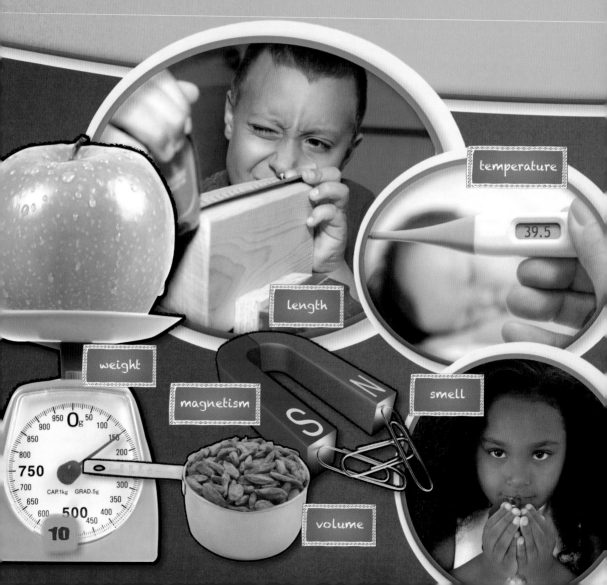

temperature

39.5

length

weight

magnetism

smell

volume

We look for a number of things when observing. But we always start with **physical properties**. These are things we can assess without altering a substance. Weight, volume, length, color, hardness, and smell are all physical properties. Magnetism is another example. So is the density of an object or how compact it is. We might even consider whether an object can conduct heat or electricity. The temperature at which a solid becomes liquid—its melting point—is another physical property. So is boiling point—when liquid becomes gas. When water turns to ice, the phase change doesn't alter its chemistry. It's still hydrogen and oxygen, just colder and solid.

It's a Phase

Chemistry has its own term for each type of phase change.

Change	Name of Change	Example
solid to liquid	melting	ice to water
liquid to gas	evaporation	water to steam
solid to gas	sublimation	dry ice to gas
gas to solid	deposition	water vapor to ice
gas to liquid	condensation	moist air to dew drops
liquid to solid	freezing	water to ice

11

Substances can also have **chemical properties**. These properties describe the substance's potential to react with something else. In other words, chemical properties tell us if a substance could be a reactant.

The chemical properties we might measure aren't standard. There isn't a set list that we check off. Rather, what we measure depends on what we want to study. Often, our focus is on whether a material will react in response to acid, water, or air.

Maybe we want to know if something is flammable. Will it burn when oxygen is present? Maybe we want to know just how flammable it is. How long will it burn? Perhaps we want to test if it will explode when ignited. We might like to see if an object will rust. Other times, the question might be if it will turn into another substance.

When observing physical properties, no changes are made to the substance. But in these examples, there is a risk of altering the original substance. It is the only way to test a substance's chemical properties. In all these cases, we are actually looking to see whether a chemical reaction will occur.

Chemical Evidence

Scientists examine chemical properties of evidence to solve crimes. They can use chemical properties to identify chemicals, poisons, or small bits of evidence left on the scene.

Creating a Product

Every chemical reaction will produce at least one new compound. This new substance is called the **product**. The product may be physically different from the original substance. And it is always, in some way, chemically changed.

When two or more elements combine to form a compound, a chemical reaction takes place. For example, hydrogen and oxygen are two reactants that combine to form water. The compound is the product, which in this case would be water. It's quite different from the two gases that combine to form it!

Compounds can also react to form a product. Take potassium iodide and lead nitrate. Both are compounds. Both are colorless liquids. Combined, they form a solid yellow substance called *lead iodide*. This new compound is the product of a chemical reaction.

Chemical reactions aren't limited to the lab. When we boil a raw egg, it transforms. The egg is chemically changed. The boiled egg is a product and will never return to its previous composition.

Likewise, when we place cookie dough in the oven, it's chemical composition changes. The baked cookies taste and smell different from the dough. These are clues that a chemical change has taken place. Our product is freshly baked cookies!

We use chemical reactions to make cars and rockets go. Rockets get their power from a chemical reaction that occurs when liquid hydrogen and liquid oxygen are combined.

Chemical Shorthand

Scientists write out reactions in symbols. They're a little like math equations. But here, the numbers become elements and compounds. First, reactants add together. Then, an arrow leads to the result. For example:

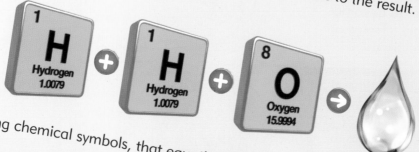

Using chemical symbols, that equation looks like this: $H_2 + O \rightarrow H_2O$.

We have to cook an egg to cause a chemical reaction. The same is true for cookies. In other words, we have to apply heat. Without heat, we would still have a raw egg and raw cookie dough.

Heat doesn't have to be there for every chemical reaction to start. But some kind of energy needs to get things going. Heat, light, and electricity can all kick-start chemical reactions. We refer to this as **activation energy**.

Activation energy starts electrons hopping. But electrons hold the atoms of the molecule together. And they can't do that if they're moving to different atoms. So, freeing the electrons means breaking the bonds between atoms. Doing so allows the electrons to form new bonds. And new bonds result in a new compound. Thus, activation energy enables a new product to form.

Sometimes, when atoms bind together, the bonds are very weak. For these bonds, not much energy is needed. The electrons start moving with very little help. For strong bonds, though, it takes a lot more activation energy to get things going.

Ionic Bonds

Atoms with only one electron in their outer layer are unstable. Unstable atoms trade electrons with each other to become stable. This is an ionic bond.

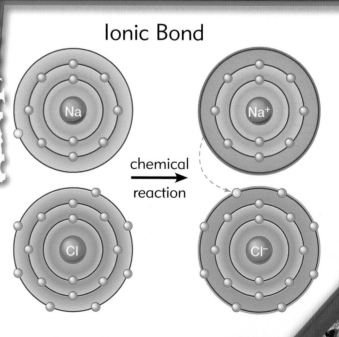

Ionic Bond

chemical reaction

Covalent Bonds

Atoms can also bond by overlapping their outer shells. Then, they share electrons rather than trade them. This is called a *covalent bond*.

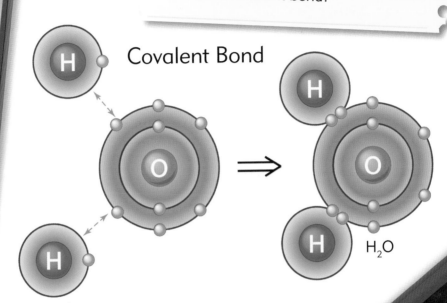

Covalent Bond

H_2O

Once started, chemical reactions can happen very fast. Take dynamite, for example. It will react with oxygen almost instantly. But that's only when there's plenty of oxygen around. Dynamite burns slowly when there is a lower concentration of oxygen.

Particle size also changes **reactivity**. The smaller a particle is, the less time the reaction takes. A powder version of a substance will react more quickly than a clump of the same material.

Temperature can affect reactivity, too. Heat speeds reaction time. Iron forms rust when it meets oxygen. But iron isn't highly reactive, so this happens slowly, over weeks or even years. Gas grills rust quickly, though. That's because the iron gets hot when the grill is used.

Iron coated with zinc will rust slowly. In this case, zinc acts as an **inhibitor**. This substance slows a reaction. It can even stop one.

On the flip side, a **catalyst** speeds up a reaction. It does so by reducing the activation energy needed. Our bodies contain natural catalysts. For example, an enzyme in our saliva speeds up starch breakdown. This catalyst helps change the food that we eat into energy that we can use.

Water must be present in the air for iron and oxygen to form rust.

rusty padlock

Cool Catalysts

Catalysts can help to speed up a reaction. When a catalyst is added to a reactant, the energy increases. The higher energy in the reaction causes the molecules to work faster—producing the product much quicker!

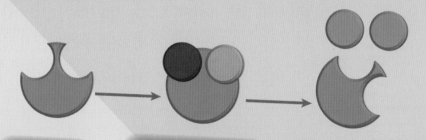

catalyst

Catalyst bonds to reactants.

Product is quickly released.

Interesting Inhibitors

Inhibitors slow and sometimes even stop chemical reactions.

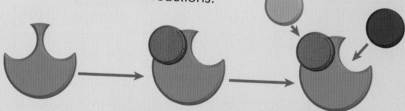

catalyst

Inhibitor bonds to catalyst.

Reactants are blocked when they try to bond to catalyst.

Categorizing Reactions

Chemical reactions fall into six main types—synthesis, decomposition, single displacement, double displacement, acid-base, and combustion.

Synthesis

The simplest type of reaction is synthesis. Here, two or more simple substances combine. When they do so, they form a more complex compound as a result.

You can combine the elements copper and sulfur using synthesis. When you do, they will form copper sulfide. This compound is the product. Something to note happens here. Extra sulfur escapes as a gas. When hot sulfur hits the air, it reacts with oxygen. A poisonous gas is created as a result. That poison isn't a product of synthesis. It's a byproduct.

A byproduct is a secondary product. It's a product that is a result of a side reaction. Every reaction type can produce these kinds of byproducts. Luckily, not all of them are poisonous.

Decomposition

The opposite of synthesis is decomposition. In these reactions, a complex substance breaks down into simpler ones. The reaction separates a substance.

For instance, you can break down water into its elements. All it takes is a push from an electric current. The water compound will be split into hydrogen and oxygen. The electric current separates the liquid. That process is called *electrolysis*. But not all decomposition occurs in this way.

Chlorophyll Camouflage

Plants make food with a form of synthesis called *photosynthesis*. They use sun, water, and carbon dioxide to synthesize chlorophyll. Chlorophyll gives leaves their green color. When the days shorten in fall, plants make less food. Without chlorophyll present, we see the natural oranges and yellows of the leaves.

Decomposition Saves Lives

Airbags in cars use decomposition to expand. They contain sodium azide pellets. When sodium azide is exposed to an electrical current, it decomposes to nitrogen gas and sodium. The nitrogen gas quickly expands and fills the airbag.

Single Displacement

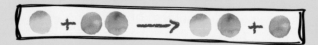

Another type of reaction is single displacement. This is sometimes called a *substitute reaction* because one item takes the place of another. In these reactions, two substances compete to bond with another substance.

For example, place an iron nail in a liquid solution of copper sulfate and watch what happens. The iron and copper compete to be part of the solution. The nail begins turning a pinkish brown color. That's because the copper is leaving the liquid compound. At the same time, the liquid turns from blue to pale green. The color change happens when the iron deposits where the copper was. Iron and copper sulfate become iron sulfate and copper.

Double Displacement

In a double-displacement reaction, there's an exchange of partners. Here, two new compounds form. This means there are two products.

Let's look at an example. If two couples are dancing together and they switch partners, this represents a double-displacement reaction. Margo and Tom are dance partners. Lucy and Andrew are a pair. As the dance progresses, a switch is made. During this switch, Margo and Andrew become partners and Lucy and Tom become partners. This switch results in two new couples. Just like in double displacement, after the switch is made, new compounds are formed.

Double the Fun

You can amaze your friends and family with the help of a double-displacement reaction. Just put baking soda into a container. Then, add a little vinegar. (Add food coloring for drama.) Watch and enjoy the fizzy fun!

pH Scale

0
1
2
3
4
5
6
7
8
9
10
11
12
13
14

Acid-Base Reaction

The baking soda in our cookies represents the base part of an acid-base reaction. That's a special kind of double displacement.

Atoms are usually neutral. They have as many electrons as they do protons. When an atom has extra or missing electrons, it becomes an ion. A substance with hydrogen ions is an acid. One with hydroxide ions is a base.

Acids can be weak—like the citric acid that makes lemons tart. Or they can be strong, like the stomach acid that digests our food. Bases also can be weak, like baking soda, or strong, like bleach.

Bath soap is a weak base that results from combining a weak acid and a strong base. Shampoo is a weak acid that results from mixing a strong acid and a weak base.

Hydrogen Power

To measure the strength of bases and acids, we use the pH scale—where the *pH* stands for the *power of hydrogen* (as in hydrogen and hydroxide ions). This scale ranges from 0 (strong acid) to 14 (strong base). Neutral substances, such as water, would rank 7 on this scale.

Combustion

Combustion reactions combine a reactant with oxygen to produce energy. In other words, they burn.

Combustion doesn't just burn wood in a fireplace to give off heat. These reactions allow us to fly to the moon! Rockets contain hydrogen gas. All it takes is a spark for hydrogen to react with oxygen. The two gases continue burning until one is gone. The energy that results is powerful enough to boost a rocket into space.

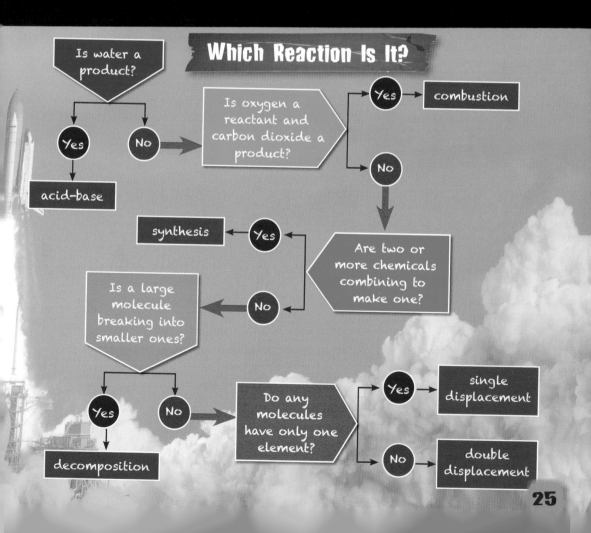

Which Reaction Is It?

Is water a product?

Yes → acid-base

No → Is oxygen a reactant and carbon dioxide a product?

Yes → combustion

No → Are two or more chemicals combining to make one?

Yes → synthesis

No → Is a large molecule breaking into smaller ones?

Yes → decomposition

No → Do any molecules have only one element?

Yes → single displacement

No → double displacement

World of Chemistry

Chemistry doesn't just happen inside a lab. And it doesn't have to be boring. Chemical reactions happen all the time. They are all around us—even inside us!

We can thank acid-base reactions for providing us with both our soap and our shampoo. Synthesis creates the water that washes them away, leaving us clean.

Double displacement gives us those fluffy pancakes we get to eat for breakfast. (When we're really lucky, that is.) And decomposition allows us to turn that yummy breakfast into brain fuel. It's how we manage to stay alert all day at school.

Baking with Chemistry

Try baking bread at home without baking soda and see what happens. Leave different things out of the recipe for different results.

Enzymes in our mouths and stomachs act as catalysts. They help us quickly break down the food into energy. And good thing, too, because combustion engines makes our cars zoom. We need lots of energy as we make our way from home to school.

Chemistry in the classroom can be just as exciting. After all, experiments are just another way to reveal the secrets of the substances that surround us.

Observing physical and chemical properties in a lab prepares us to observe those same things in the real world. Because the real world is a world full of chemistry!

Think Like a Scientist

How can you tell if a combination causes a chemical reaction? Experiment and find out!

What to Get

- 3 clear cups
- hot water
- powdered laundry detergent
- purple cabbage
- sealable bags
- spoon
- vinegar

What to Do

1 Place 5–10 purple cabbage leaves into a sealable bag. Fill the bag halfway with hot water. Zip the bag tightly, and squish the ingredients together until you have cabbage juice.

2 Fill each cup halfway with the cabbage juice. Try to avoid pouring in big chunks of cabbage. Add a spoonful of vinegar into the first cup. Observe what happens, and record the results.

3 Add a spoonful of powdered laundry detergent to the second. Observe what happens, and record the results.

4 Add a spoonful of water to the third cup. Watch what happens, and record the results. What kind of change resulted from each ingredient? How do you know?

Glossary

-base—a double-displacement
reaction with acid and base
reactants

vation energy—the energy
necessary to get a chemical reaction
tarted

roduct—something that is
produced during the production or
destruction of something else

lyst—a substance that causes a
chemical reaction to happen more
quickly

nical change—a change that
results in a new substance

nical properties—characteristics of
matter that can be observed during
a chemical change

nical reaction—a change that
results in a new substance

bustion—a chemical reaction that
occurs when oxygen combines with
other substances to produce heat
and usually light

pound—a substance made of two
or more types of atoms bonded
together

mposition—a reaction that breaks
down a complex substance into
simpler ones

double displacement—a displacement
reaction with an exchange of
compound partners

element—a basic substance that is
made of atoms of only one kind
and cannot be separated by
ordinary chemical means into
simpler substances

inhibitor—a substance that slows or
interferes with a chemical reaction

physical change—a change that does
not form a new substance

physical properties—traits which can
be used to describe and identify an
object, such as color, length, and
boiling point

product—the result of a chemical
reaction, chemically distinct from
the reactants

reactants—substances that change
when combined with other
substances in a chemical reaction

reactivity—the tendency of a substance
to change when mixed with another
substance

single displacement—a reaction in
which one substance substitutes
another in a compound

synthesis—a reaction combining
simple substances into a more
complex product